"I just finished re-reading the *Cold Mountain* poems. I love where they put your head." PENELOPE ROSE, staff, Pier 5 Law Offices, San Francisco

"This translation of *Cold Mountain Transcendental Poetry* is Wandering Poet's gift to the Western world. We are greatly enriched by it." J. TONY SERRA, counter culture lawyer, San Francisco

"Reading *Cold Mountain Transcendental Poetry* is a wonderful spiritual experience that I highly recommend." GRANDMASTER BILL DEWART, 9th dan, San Francisco Academy of Tae Kwan Do

"Wandering Poet takes us to Han Shan's Cold Mountain: a place in the heart. It's a book to read and re-read." TOM GOLDWASSER, antiquarian book dealer, San Francisco

"I am really enjoying and learning from the *Cold Mountain Transcendental Poetry*....Thank you!" MALCOLM GUITE, Cambridge

"I love having this book of poems in my Kindle. When I am in a doctor's waiting room, or relaxing at Starbuck's, or calming down from a stressful day, or any time I need a mini-getaway, I read these poems. They transport me to another time and place, a place of peace, a place where I can contemplate eternity. I love the story of how the poems were found written on rocks on a mountain top in China. For a moment I can be on that mountain top with the hermit of long ago. JANET MEANS, storyteller, Phoenix

"Please be our featured poet and read from *Cold Mountain*." PHILLIP HACKETT, North Beach Poets Gallery, San Francisco

"Reading these poems takes me to Cold Mountain." JOHN ALLRED, fine art consultant, Cotati, CA

"I am impressed with the quality of these translations of *Cold Mountain Transcendental Poetry* by Wandering Poet. They are the most accurate of all the English translations available. Moreover, they capture the spirit of the originals, which no other English translation does. In a few of the poems, I like the translation better than the original, the word play, the metaphor, the spirit of the poem. Wandering Poet has done a great service with this translation. I highly recommend *Cold Mountain Transcendental Poetry* translated by Wandering Poet. It is and will remain the go to collection for lovers of the Cold Mountain poetry." YAO XIAO YING, M.S., San Francisco

"I found that reading these transcendental poems was very peaceful. When you are looking for deeper meaning in your life *Cold Mountain* is the perfect book to help you find it." PAIGE LOVITT, ReaderViews.com

"This is the most accurately and carefully translated version of this beautiful collection of poetry available. It REALLY captures the feeling, word-play and rhythm of the original work much better than other translations. Enjoy!" VERSE LOVER, amazon review

寒山

COLD MOUNTAIN
Transcendental Poetry
by the T'ang Zen Poet Han-shan

COLD MOUNTAIN

Transcendental Poetry
by the T'ang Zen Poet Han-shan

100 Poems
translated by
Wandering Poet, M.A.

Gone Fishin' Press

Copyright © 2005, 2007, 2008, 2011, 2012, 2015
by Wandering Poet
all rights reserved
Seventh Edition
Revised and Expanded
ISBN-13: 978-0692510797
ISBN-10: 0692510796
Library of Congress Control Number: 2015913161
Buddha of Compassion, San Francisco California

Calligraphy by Hua Tao Bao

COVER: *Hanshan & Shihte,*
"We chew magic mushrooms beneath the pines"
Indara Yintuoluo c. 1375, Tokyo National Museum

The source for this English translation is

Cold Mountain Poems & Notes
(with Lost Poetry Notes)

Containing 313 Cold Mountain Poems
57 Pick-up Poems
6 Big-stick Poems

by
Xiang Chu

Zhonghua Book Company
Beijing, China

ISBN 978-7101-01645-1

© 1997, 2000, 2010
3rd edition

Cold Mountain
Sheng Mou 1350

The poems marked with one star * are literal translations, word for word, to show the playful childlike quality of the originals. A few of these literal translations also have my own rendering somewhere in the book. You must discover these surprises for yourself!

The poems marked with two stars ** are by Cold Mountain's friend Pick-up.

The poems marked with three stars *** are attributed to Pick-up but appear to me to be authored by Cold Mountain.

The two poems marked with four stars **** are traditionally a single 14 line poem. However, in my view, it reads better as two separate poems.

The quotations from the poems in the following introduction are from this translation, unless marked as poems by Burton Watson in his book, *Cold Mountain: 100 poems by the T'ang poet Han-shan*, (1970) Columbia University Press, i.e., (W1). Watson's book contains many of the biographical poems, which this 'transcendental' collection does not.

INTRODUCTION

"If the reader wishes to know the biography of Han-Shan, he must deduce it from the poems themselves." [Burton Watson, Cold Mountain: 100 Poems by the T'ang poet Han-shan, (1970) Columbia University Press.]

No one knows who wrote the Cold Mountain poetry, though it has inspired the poets of many generations and cultures. The Cold Mountain poet is revered in Japan, where he is known as Kanzan. I first discovered the Cold Mountain poetry from seeing it mentioned by a favorite Japanese poet, Ryokan:

> *All day I walk in the forest gathering food*
> *At dusk I enter my hut and close the door behind me*
> *I kindle a fire with branches still bearing dried leaves*
> *Quietly I read the poems from Cold Mountain*
> *A rising west wind brings rain sweeping across the land*
> *My little hut creaks and moans under the hand of the storm*
> *But stretched serene upon the floor I breathe and listen to the rain*
> *There is not a doubt in my heart or a worry to disturb my mind*

I reasoned that if Ryokan so enjoyed Cold Mountain poetry, it must be very special. So I went in search of some to read. And that led to a life-long affair with Cold Mountain.

Jack Kerouac dedicated his book **Dharma Bums** to the Cold Mountain poet and introduced his poetry to a generation of Americans. Today the Cold Mountain poet is probably the best known of all the Buddhist poets to the American audience. Yet, we really know nothing of the author except what we can learn from the poems themselves.

The poems were found written on the rocks in a remote region in China's Tien Tai Mountains, on the coast south of Shanghai and Hangchou. They tell the story of a gentle recluse, born in the T'ang Dynasty, more than a thousand years ago, and of his long life in the mountains as a "guest" of Nature, living in a cave and foraging for food.

The poems tell us that he began life in a good family. "My father and mother left me a good living; I need not envy the fields of other men." (W1) He was a scholar, educated in history, the classics and mathematics. "In vain I slaved to understand the **Three Histories**; Uselessly I pored over the **Five Classics**." (W30) He was privileged and widely traveled. "I think of all the places I've been, Chasing about from one famous spot to another." (W37)

He was a musician. "I feasted with friends in Chrysanthemum Valley, Carried my lute to Peacock Isle." He was trained in calligraphy and the arts: "I mastered every one of the Six Arts [etiquette, music, archery, charioteering, calligraphy and mathematics]." (W14) He was proud of his mastery, "Boasting, my brushwork is strong."

He was trained in martial arts and weapons, familiar with the use of sword, bow and crossbow. "I was a student with books and sword...I studied the arts of peace and the arts of war; the arts of war and the arts of peace." (W33) He served in the military. "I fought in the west but won no medals." (W33) After his military service, he worked for a while as a clerk or bookkeeper, "Until I'm old I'll go on checking census figures; As in the past, a petty clerk scribbling in tax ledgers." (W30) He became frustrated and discouraged at being passed over repeatedly, because of a handicap, or possibly a war injury, for civil service positions he was well qualified for. "I'm not so bad at reports and decisions, Why can't I get ahead in the government?" (W19)

Finally, he quit competing and striving. He married, moved to a remote farm at the edge of the forest, where "I pick wild fruit in hand with my child, Till the hillside field with my wife." (W2) He became a farmer and raised a family. "Clack clack my wife works her loom, Jabber jabber goes my son at play...Who comes to commend me on my way of life? Well, the woodcutter sometimes passes by." (W1)

He loved books. "I took along books when I hoed the fields." (W32) He always lived among piles of books. "And in my house what do I have? Only a bed piled high with books." (W1) All his life, to the very end, even while living with the elements at Cold Mountain, he always had books. "One or two heavenly books I read, mumbling, beneath the pines." He describes himself as simple, quiet, honest, straightforward and lazy.

Up to this point his life can be compared to that of any well born modern youth. He was privileged, educated, traveled, served in the military, went to war, came home to seek a good job, married and began to raise a family.

But as the years pass, the poet becomes unhappy and dissatisfied with his life. "Why am I always so depressed? I am filled with sadness, A sadness I can hardly endure." (W36) He leaves home and family behind, packs up some books and begins to wander. "Now I've broken my ties with the world of red dust, I spend my time wandering and read all I want." (W32) He experiences a growing sense that life has been wasted, that life has passed him by and nothing has been accomplished. "With a heart full of doubt and regret, A life has passed and nothing is accomplished."

He becomes increasingly lonely. In the modern world, he sees selfishness and greed, ignorance and corruption. Nothing has changed in a thousand years. Disappointed with life and his fellow man, he becomes withdrawn, sinks into poverty and depression. Even the rats scorn his condition, as they prowl in search of crumbs. "Since I lost the brindle cat, the rats come right up and peer into the empty pot." (W24)

In this low state, he turns his back on the civilized world and goes to live out his remaining years in solitude in the mountains as a hermit, "Why am I always so depressed? What shall I do? Say, what shall I do? Take this old body home and hide it in the mountains." (W36)

He settles at a remote place called Cold Mountain, where "I gather leaves and thatch a hut among the pines, dig a pond and lead a trickle from the brook." He plants a small vegetable garden. But a hut and garden require maintenance. When the hut turns gray with age and falls apart, and "Weeds fill the garden, New vines climb and hang everywhere, Monkeys strip the trees of mountain fruit, Egrets and cranes eat all the pond fish," he moves to a large no maintenance cave at the base of a cliff high on the south face of Cold Mountain. His distant view of the world of men is often hidden when the mountain becomes shrouded in mist and cloud. "Cold Mountain is hidden in white clouds, It's peaceful to be cut off from the busy world."

With his growing knowledge of herb lore, he no longer bothers to tend a garden, but relies increasingly on foraging. A garden requires constant attention. Foraging requires only that you have a basket and know when and where to look when things are ready to harvest. "Carrying a basket I gather mountain mushrooms, Carrying a bucket I return with fruit." You let Nature take care of the planting, weeding and watering. This approach calls for an intimate knowledge of the land and the things that grow there, and confidence that Nature will provide for your needs. "Since I came to Cold

Mountain, I've lived by eating mountain fruits, What is there to worry about?"

Finally, the poet comes to look on Nature as his host and himself as Nature's "guest." He now takes his food entirely from the forest, living in the clouds as a hermit poet, harvesting and dining on 'mountain fruit.' "Here I lay out a handful of mountain fruit...Rushes serve in place of a mat, A plantain leaf will do for a plate."

"Mountain fruit" is his metaphor for the generosity of Nature, for the variety of wild edibles that make up his diet, the ferns and other wild greens, assorted mushrooms, wild plums, cherries, peaches, olives, plantains and other fruits, bamboo shoots, edible roots, medicinal herbs. These and more are mentioned in the poems.

The poet uses words in the poems that distinguish a variety of uses for mushrooms. With his knowledge of herb lore, he uses mushrooms as food, medicine, spiritual sacrament and longevity herb. The words "mountain mushrooms" in the poems are a generic term meaning all mushrooms. But the poet and his friend, Pick-up, both use the words "magic mushrooms" in a number of poems. "Come sit with me among the white clouds, I will teach you a magic mushroom song."

The words "magic mushroom" appear in old Chinese texts on herb lore and medicine and refer to *ganoderma lucidum*, the reishi mushroom, which has been one of the most revered herbs in the Chinese pharmacopoeia for 5000 years. Traditionally this mushroom is used to promote healthy immune system, heart and liver function, and as a general health tonic. The reishi is not commonly known as an hallucinogen or "magic mushroom." Though, according to mushroom expert, Dr. Terry Willard, author of **Reishi Mushroom: Herb of Spiritual Potency and Medical Wonder,** when the reishi mushroom is found growing on a *mimosa* tree, it becomes a powerful hallucinogen, or "magic mushroom." The bark and root bark from the mimosa is known to contain as much as 2-3% of a psychedelic alkaloid, DMT, which can be extracted and used in its pure form. Apparently, the reishi mushroom is also capable of extracting the DMT. The *mimosa* tree grows in abundance in the mountains where Han-shan lived.

Hallucinogenic or "magic mushrooms" have been used by shamans, poets and heaven seekers across the ages, as a stimulant to energize the nervous system, sharpen the senses, clean the lenses, enhance the practice of meditation, induce peak experience, produce visions. It seems clear the Cold Mountain poet and his friend Pick-up shared in this tradition.

The poet lived a very long life in his cave on Cold Mountain. In one poem he says he is more than 70, in another that he is one hundred, and in yet another that he is more than one hundred years old. "Old and sick, more than one hundred years, Face haggard, hair white, I'm happy to still live in the mountains, A cloth covered phantom watching the years flow by." He may have lived to be one hundred twenty. One poem indicates that he may have retired to Cold Mountain while still in his 30s. "Thirty years ago I was born into the world...And today I've come home to Cold Mountain." If true, this means that he spent between 70 and 90 years living on Cold Mountain as Nature's "guest."

His main preoccupations seem to be reading ancient texts, laughing, singing, dancing, writing poems on the rocks, taking long leisurely walks to explore the terrain and to gather food and firewood, or to visit his friends, Big-stick and Pick-up, two poet monks who lived at Kuoching Temple, a day's walk from his cave on Cold Mountain. These are the only close friends the poet mentions in the poems. Both sometimes make the climb to visit him at home in his cave.

Once settled at Cold Mountain, it quickly becomes clear in the poetry that the poet has left the world behind. He has transcended the civilized world and is now in heaven, at one with his wild surroundings. For the first time in his life he is completely happy and at peace. He becomes like a child. The poems are simple and direct, yet majestic. They reflect a new state of mind and have the power to lift the reader to share a moment in the poet's heaven.

The poetry is rich with metaphor. In Buddhist literature, the word **"mountain"** can be a metaphor for heaven, or enlightenment. In the Cold Mountain poetry, the poet uses the words **"Cold Mountain"** to refer to the place where he lives; but also to heaven, to a state of mind, to himself, and to the poetry. You may read all these meanings in the words **"Cold Mountain."**

Similarly, leaning on the **"rock"** or **"cliff"** are metaphors for the truth on which he depends. His companions, **"tigers & deer,"** are the dangers and joys of life. Look for metaphor in the poems and your reading will be rewarded.

Altogether, there are 313 Cold Mountain poems, plus 9 poems that are attributed to the poet's friend, Pick-up, but appear to me to be authored by Cold Mountain, for a total of 322. Within the total number of Cold Mountain poems, there are three distinct groups: the biographical poems, about the poet's life before he arrived at Cold Mountain; religious and political poems, generally critical of conventional wisdom and those who embrace it; and the transcendental poems, written during his sojourn at Cold Mountain. This seventh edition collection of 100 poems contains all of the transcendental poems, and none of the biographical, religious or political poems.   For a good selection of the biographical poems, see Burton Watson.

For their assistance in understanding Han-shan's reference to medicinal and psychoactive mushrooms, thanks go to Dr. Michael McCulloch, Pine Street Chinese Clinic, San Anselmo, California, and Dr. Terry Willard, mushroom authority.

These translations are completely accurate, the very best you will find in English, they are rich with metaphor, and the poetry is close to the heart of Cold Mountain. Happy reading!

Wandering Poet
Cold Mountain, California
Summer 2015

Cold Mountain & Pick-up
Hashimoto Gaho 1835-1908

the poems

There is a Precious Mountain
Even the Seven Treasures cannot compare
A cold moon rises through the pines
Layer upon layer of bright clouds
How many towering peaks?
How many wandering miles?
The valley streams run clear
Happiness Forever!

Among a thousand clouds and ten thousand streams
Here lives an idle man
In the day time wandering over green mountains
At night coming home to sleep by the cliff
Swiftly springs and autumns pass
But my mind is at peace, clear and free
By now I need nothing to lean on
To be still as the waters of the autumn river

I dreamed a place where I have come to dwell
Cold Mountain says it all
Monkeys scream, the valley fog is cold
My bamboo gate blends with the color of the peaks
I gather leaves and thatch a hut among the pines
Dig a pond and lead a trickle from the brook
Long ago I left the world behind
Eating ferns, I pass the years in peace

Cold Mountain is hidden in white clouds
It's peaceful to be cut off from the busy world
I use dry grass for cushions in my mountain home
My only light is the round moon
My bed is the rock beside the green pool
Tigers and deer are my companions
I delight in this happy peaceful life
Forever beyond the world of men

I settled at Cold Mountain long ago
Already it seems like ages
Wandering free I roam the woods and streams
Lingering to watch things be themselves
Men don't come this far into the mountains
Where white clouds gather and billow
Dry grass makes a comfortable mattress
The blue sky is a fine quilt
Happy to pillow my head on the rock
I leave heaven and earth to endless change

Today I sat before the cliff
Until the mist and rainbows disappeared
I followed the emerald stream
Explored a thousand tiers of green cliffs
In the morning my spirit rests among white clouds
At night a bright moon floats in the sky
I am free of the busy world
There is not a doubt in my heart or a worry to
disturb my mind

Born 30 years ago
I've wandered ten thousand miles
Through the green grass by the edge of the stream
Beyond the border across the desert of red dust
I picked purple fungus to become immortal
Studied and became a learned man
Today I've come home to Cold Mountain
To be a hermit and forget the affairs of the world

***

A cold moon rises through the pines
Layer upon layer of bright clouds
Tier on tier of towering peaks
You can see a thousand miles
Pools of water crystal clear
Moonlight shining in the mirror
This precious Mountain Temple
Even the Seven Treasures cannot compare

Cold Mountain and Pick-up

A fellow who enjoys pink clouds
Lives away from the crowd
He's very wise
In summer as well as autumn
The green stream bubbles musically
Wind rustles the tall pines
One can sit half a day
Forgetting the worries of a hundred years

My hut is at the foot of a green cliff
Weeds fill the garden
New vines climb and hang everywhere
Ancient rocks form tall cliffs
Monkeys strip the trees of mountain fruit
Egrets and cranes eat all the pond fish
One or two heavenly books
I read mumbling beneath the pines

Roosting beneath Cold Cliff
Is a mystery full of surprise
Carrying a basket I gather mountain mushrooms
Carrying a bucket I return with fruit
Spreading a vegetarian meal I sit in my hut
Smack smack chewing magic mushrooms
Rinsing clean the ladle and bowl
Mixing together a thin stew
Sitting in the evening sun clutching my robe
Leisurely I read ancient poems

I'm happy in the every day way
Among the mist and vines and caves
The wilderness is boundless
My companions are lazy white clouds
There are roads but they do not reach the world
My mind has come to rest and nothing can
                                  stir my thought
On a bed of rock, I sit, alone in the night
While a round moon climbs up Cold Mountain

Since I came to Cold Mountain I forgot everything
Nothing worries me anymore
In leisure I write poems on the rocks
Following my karma, drifting like an untied boat

In leisure I went to the mountain top
The sun shines sparkling bright
I look around
White clouds and cranes are flying by

I love the joy of mountains
Wandering free with no concerns
Every day I find food for this crippled body
There's leisure for thinking, nothing to do
Often I carry an ancient book
Sometimes I climb a rock pavilion
To look down a thousand foot precipice
Overhead are swirling clouds
A cold moon chilly cold
My body feels like a flying crane

***

Woods and streams always make me smile
No smoke from the fires of men for many miles
Clouds drift among the rocky peaks
Rushing waterfalls plunge down the gorge
The song of apes rings through the forest
A tiger's roar echoes over all
A soft breeze rustles the fragrant pines
Birds are in conversation everywhere
Wandering, I follow the stream
Alone, I climb the heights
Often I sit cross-legged on the rock
Or lie gazing up at hanging vines
But when I see a distant town
All I hear is noise and confusion

****

My Cold Mountain home has a dry roof
This cave is perfect, no leaks
No wind can move it
Everything I once knew has been left behind
The stillness here is precious
There is no one to gossip and chatter
A round moon shines in the night sky
The bright sun shines in the daytime
Don't call me to famous religious spots
I'm happy here

****

The earth has famous officials
And don't forget the Emperor's men
But I wander free on Cold Mountain
Happy and singing and laughing

In Cold Mountain house
There are no walls inside
Its doors are the six directions
The roof is the blue blue sky
Room after empty room
East wall meets west wall
There is nothing between
People feel deprived with nothing
When it's cold I make a fire
When hungry I cook some vegetables
Those who learned to plow
Increase their crops, increase their wealth
Their karma leads to hell
And it lasts a long long time
But if you think good thoughts
You will understand the truth

Cold Mountain reaches to the clouds
From peaks high in the sky I can see far below
Heaven's pagoda floats above a green ridge
An ancient temple rests among the rainbows
At Cold Mountain Gate wind rustles the tall pines
God's Footpath is lost among the foggy cliffs
In the blue sky a thousand mountains appear
Deep gorges wander like tangled vines

I see the top of Cold Mountain
Alone high above the rest of the peaks
Wind rustles the pines and bamboo
The moon and the tides come and go
I look down far below the green mountain
I discuss Tao with the clouds
I happily enjoy the mountains and waters
My whole being admires the teachings of Tao

Sea of Cloud
Huang Chun Pi 1898

When hermits hide from the world
Many retire to the mountains
Green vines grow thick
Beside the bubbling streams
Foggy foggy quiet and peaceful
Reaching reaching happiness and leisure
Events of the world do not reach the mountains
A peaceful heart is clear as a white lotus

Deer live deep in the forest
They drink water and eat grass
Stretch out and sleep under a tree
Lovely they have no worries or cares
Then you have wealthy families
The rich food they eat is never enough
Their lives are filled with worry and sorrow
Who has the better life?

The paths I walked in the old times
Now 70 years have gone
I've had no contact with the past
I've buried myself in this mountain home
Now my hair and beard are white
I still stay in these cloud wrapped mountains
For the sake of those who follow
Why not study the words of the ancients?

Since I came to Cold Mountain
I've passed many winters and springs
One gets old while the mountains and waters
                        do not change
I've seen many generations come and go

I live on a mountain
People don't know
Among white clouds
Forever at peace

Cold Mountain son
Forever unchanged
I live alone
Beyond life and death

Cold Mountain is a quiet place
Seldom do men of the world pass
Often you meet forest birds
And together sing mountain songs
Wild fruits grow in the valleys
Old pines cover the mountain cliffs
Here you see a wanderer
Resting on the mountain trail

Cold Mountain Trail
(detail) Sheng Mou 1350

What is the saddest thing in the world?
Hurry hurry hurry chasing desire
Don't learn from the white cloud mountain man
One layer of shabby clothing is my entire wealth
In autumn I watch the leaves fall
In spring I watch the trees flower
I sleep through heaven and earth with no concerns
With the bright moon and gentle breeze I dwell

Tier on tier of beautiful mountains and streams
Blue green vistas locked in white clouds
The mist makes my bandana wet
Dew coats my grass cape
My feet climb in straw sandals
In my hand an old wooden stick
When I gaze down again on the busy world
It has become a land of phantoms and dreams to me

When I see my reflection in the green stream
Or sitting on the rock leaning against the cliff
My heart is like a cloud with no earthly connection
Why worry about earthly things?

My heart is like an autumn moon
The green stream runs clear and clean
What can compare?
What more can I say?

The mountains are very cold
From ancient times
Tiers of mountains covered with snow
Silent, shrouded thick with fog
When grass first sprouts, spring is already gone
Leaves fall before autumn arrives
Here stands a wanderer lost
Who looks but cannot see the sky

The ages pass and worries too
Spring arrives; everything is fresh
Mountain flowers and streams are happy together
Steep cliffs dance in the green mist
Bees and butterflies are happy together
Fish and birds are especially happy
Friends play together never tiring
Come the dawn I still cannot sleep

Even with the fastest ship
Or riding a thousand mile horse
You cannot reach my home
People say the place is secluded and wild
A rock cave deep in the mountains
Clouds and thunder all day long
I am not Confucius
My words you will not understand

Cold Mountain is very deep
No one walks this road
Tier on tier of lazy white clouds
On the green ridge a lone ape howls
I have no worries or concerns
Polishing my character still suits my old age
My appearance changes winter and summer
But my heart and mind remain the same

Tiers of mountains and clouds reach the blue sky
The road is narrow, the forest deep, there is no traffic
From far you can see the toad in the moon
Close you can hear birdsong twitter twitter
One old man sits alone on a green cliff
Living in leisure, letting his hair turn white
Sighing for yesterday and today
Mindless as water running east

Those with a warped character
Who think they have achieved something
When alive your body has limits
When dead you're a nameless ghost
From ancient times there are many like these
Why do you still struggle?
Come sit with me among the white clouds
I will teach you a magic mushroom song

*How many people in these mountains
Don't recognize Cold Mountain?
They don't know his true wisdom
They call his words gibberish*

***

The teachings of the old ones are like cold wine
The more you drink the clearer your mind
I live on Cold Mountain
Not even the shadow of a fool will you find here
I wander among caves and deep gorges
I don't keep up with worldly affairs
I have no worries, no concerns
I live far beyond shame and glory

When people see Cold Mountain
They all say he's crazy
He's nothing to look at
He wears shabby clothes
He doesn't understand our language
His words we won't repeat
To those who come and go
Come face Cold Mountain

How wonderful is Cold Mountain
Climbers are all afraid
The moon shines on clear water twinkle twinkle
Wind rustles the bamboo
Plum trees flower in the snow
Bare twisted trees have clouds for foliage
A touch of rain brings it all alive
Unless your vision is clear do not approach

Cold Mountain road is funny
No tracks of carts or horses
Ten thousand streams don't know that they sing
Tiers of mountains don't know their own weight
A thousand different grasses weep with dew
You can hear the wind in the pines
Here if you lose your way
Your body must ask your spirit for directions

My home is very hidden
Where I live there is no dust
Step in the grass, the trails go everywhere
Look up, clouds for neighbors
For music, there are birds
Ask for sermons, there is no one here
Ancient Bodhi Tree
How many years become one spring?

Climb the steep Cold Mountain way
Roads to Cold Mountain are many and never ending
The valleys are long and deep, the peaks piled high
The streams are wide, the grass is thick
The moss is slippery though there is no rain
The pines sigh though there is no wind
Who can escape the snares of the world
And come to sit with me among the white clouds?

***

Tier upon tier of mountains and clouds
Beyond the trails where men tread
The pure emerald stream holds many sights
And the bird song always agrees with my heart

I hear birds playing and singing
Lying inside my grass hut
Cherry blossoms are pink happy happy
Willow trees stand swaying in the breeze
The rising sun swallows emerald cliffs
Clouds wash the clear green pool
Whoever wants to leave the dusty world
Go up the south face of Cold Mountain

Since I retired to Cold Mountain
I've lived by eating mountain fruits
What is there to worry about?
Life passes according to karma
The months pass like a flowing stream
Days and nights like sparks from flint
Heaven and earth endlessly change
While I sit happily among these cliffs

**

I wander into Cold Mountain cave
To visit someone people don't know
Cold Mountain is my friend
We chew magic mushrooms beneath the pines
We talk of current and ancient events
We see the world as stupid and crazy
Each and every one is hell bound
Will they ever be free?

Cold Mountain & Pick-up
"We chew magic mushrooms beneath the pines."
Indara Yintuoluo c. 1375

**

Pick-up is really a pick-up
It's not just a casual name
There is no close family
Cold Mountain is my brother
Our two hearts are alike
We can discuss everything together
If you ask how many years?
Since the Yellow River ran clear

If you discuss happiness forever
It only happens to hermits
Forest flowers shine like silk
The four seasons' colors are always new
Leaning against the rock I sit
Gazing at the moon
Though I am happy here
I think of the miserable world down below

This mountain guest with quiet heart
Often sighs for the passing years
Diligently collecting vegetables and fruit
Searching endlessly for heaven
In my living room clouds begin to roll
In the forest a round moon shines bright
Why do I not go back?
The perfume of the sweet olive trees keeps me here

The intelligent don't want me
The stupid I don't want them
Fools or wise men
I no longer communicate with them
At night I sing to the bright moon
In the morning I dance with white clouds
To still my busy mouth and hands
I sit quietly with my windblown hair

Above the sky beyond the world
Cloud Road wanders
Waterfalls drop ten thousand feet
Like ribbons of silk
In the world below are sad hearts
Between is Destiny Bridge
Staunch guardian of the truth
Cold Mountain is unrivaled

Where I wander and play and rest
The mystery is difficult to describe
Without wind the vines move by themselves
Without any fog the bamboo groves are dark
Why do the bubbling streams sing?
Or clouds suddenly gather and billow?
Sitting in the forest in the afternoon
Why do I feel the warmth of the sun?

When fools read my poems
They don't understand and condemn me
When average people read my poems
They "ooh" and "aah" and call them profound
When enlightened people read my poems
They burst out smiling with bright faces
Like a young man seeing a young woman
One glance and they understand the mystery

Cold Mountain is very precious
White clouds gather and billow
The monkey's chatter makes walking happy
The tiger's roar carries above the forest
Singing the rock is smooth and good for walking
Humming alone the vines are good for climbing
Softly softly wind in the pines
Coo coo coo sound the birds

High on the mountain top
I can see to every horizon
Sitting alone where no one knows
A lone moon is reflected in the cold stream
The moon is not in the stream
The moon is in the sky
I am singing this song
In this song there is no Zen

My house does not have painted beams
The green forest is my home
A lifetime just passed by
I accomplished nothing in the busy world
Climbing, there is no easy path
Drifting, in ruin I pick flowers
If today I don't put down good roots
When will I ever see any fruit?

I've been wanting to visit East Cliff
It has been many years
Yesterday I finally went and began climbing
Halfway up I was stopped by wind and fog
The path became narrow, snagging my clothes
The moss was too slippery, I could go no further
So I lay down beneath a fragrant tree
Pillowed my head on a cloud and went to sleep

I have heard that in Tien Tai Mountains
There are precious trees
I always say I will go up Tien Tai
But the way is narrow and precarious
In this life my karma is difficult
Sighing, it will soon be over
Today I look into a mirror
Thin wisps of snow white hair

Nothing to do, I went to visit an old monk
Ten thousand tiers of smoky mountains
The old one himself pointed the way home
The round moon hangs like a lantern

My home is in the mountains
Cloud Road is hidden in mist and fog, no one comes here
Mile high cliffs deep enough to hide
Ten thousand streams, a thousand mountain peaks
Cloth bandana and wooden clogs follow the stream
Cotton robe and walking stick circle the mountain
My whole life before Cold Mountain was for nothing
Leisure and happiness are the real treasures

I live alone beneath tall cliffs
Birds fly here but no signs of people
My cave is empty, nothing inside
White clouds gently hug the peaks
Living here these many years
I always see spring and winter change
Send word to wealthy families with incense burners
What good are fame and fortune?

Kanzan & Jittoku
Kaihoku Yusho 1533-1610

I see people in the world
They are born and they die
Yesterday I was sixteen
A young man with healthy chi, strong chest
Now I'm more than seventy years
Strength faded, appearance haggard
Just like spring day flowers
Open at dawn, gone by night

Wandering among white clouds
There's no need to buy the mountains
Going down is dangerous, need a walking stick
Going up is dangerous, need a vine to hold
Along the streams, the pines are always green
Along the valleys, the rocks are many colors
Though my friends and family are all gone
Spring always comes and the birds sing

At dusk I went down the west side of the mountain
Grass and trees are emerald green
Often there are shadow places
Pines and vines grow thick
Here there are crouching tigers
They see me, hackles rise, ears go back
My hand has no weapon
I struggle to conquer my fear

If you want to know the difference between life and death
You can compare it to ice and water
Ice thawed becomes water
Water frozen becomes ice
Death is followed by rebirth
Birth is followed by death
Ice and water don't harm each other
Life and death are both beautiful

My home is in a cave
A cave that's empty with nothing inside
Clean clear empty echo echo
Nothing in here but the morning sun
A vegetable meal nourishes this weak old body
I am a cloth-covered phantom
Let your thousand sages appear
I am pure as a Buddha

I recall the places I've been
Places popular for great scenery
On Jade Mountain I climbed ten thousand peaks
On Wide Water I sailed a thousand ships
I feasted with guests in Chrysanthemum Valley
Carried my guitar to Peacock Isle
How could I know I'd wind up under a pine tree
Hugging my knees in the cold shiver shiver

***

I laugh at myself, an old man with faded health
I'm still partial to pine cliffs, I love to play alone
I sigh for the years that are gone
Following my karma, drifting like an untied boat

Old and sick, more than one hundred years
Face haggard, hair white, I'm happy to still
                live in the mountains
A cloth covered phantom watching the years flow by
Why envy people with clever ways of living?

Thousand year old rock worn smooth by ancient feet
Over a ten thousand foot cliff an empty path
A bright moon shines clean and clear
No need to ask the way

***

There are ten million scriptures
Anxious to learn you will not understand
If you want a friend and confidant
Go into Tien Tai mountains
Sit deep among the cliffs
We can discuss the ten million scriptures
But don't look for me
All you will see is a thousand mountains

People ask the way to Cold Mountain
Roads do not go through
Summer arrives yet the ice has not melted
Though the sun is out it's foggy and dim
How did I arrive here?
My mind and yours are not the same
When our minds are one
You will be here too

Stars fill the sky deep into the night
The round moon is my only light
All worldly attachments are gone
My heart is in the sky

*

I live mountain
Not people know
White cloud middle
Always peace

Kanzan & Jittoku
Kano Sansetsu 1589-1651

*

Tiers of mountains
Cold wind feet
Not need fan
Ice cold through
Moon shines bright
Mist covers everything
Sit all alone
One old man

*

Cold Mountain cold
Ice freezes rock
Mountains are green
Snow is white
Sun shines bright
Everything melt
Everything warm
Warms old man

*

Cold Mountain deep
Suits my heart
Rocks are white
Not gold
Stream water loud
Sounds like music
Your heart same
You hear music

*

Cold Mountain Road
No one comes
If can come
You number one
Cicadas sing sing
Crows caw caw
Yellow leaves fall
White clouds sweep
Rock plenty rock
Mystery Mountain

*

I live alone
Known good guy
Look careful look
Why good guy?

I live alone
I'm known as a good guy
Take a careful look
Why am I a good guy?

*

Cold Mountain son
Forever not change
Self live alone
Beyond life death

*

Often sit alone happy happy
Thoughts somewhat far gone gone
Clouds circle mountain soft soft
Wind through valley swish swish
Ape in tree bounce bounce
Bird in forest chirp chirp
Time turns hair gray gray
Winter is here sad sad

*

Remote remote Cold Mountain road
Cold cold ice cold cliff
Chirp chirp often many birds
Lone lone no sign people
Swish swish breeze blow face
Gentle gentle snow settle head
Day day no see sun
Year year no see spring

Kanzan and Jittoku
Ito Jakuchu, c. 1763

I have one robe
It's not silk... it's not satin
If you ask what color
It's not red... it's not purple
In summer it's clothing
In winter it's a blanket
I use it interchangeably winter or summer
That's the way all year long

Cold Mountain road is very remote
Cold Mountain cliffs are icy cold
I always hear singing birds
But no signs of people anywhere
A soft breeze caresses my face
Gently the snow settles on my head
Day after day I see no sun
Year after year I see no spring

When you live on Cold Mountain long enough
the autumns pass quickly
When you live alone you have no worries
When you leave the doors open no one bothers you
The bubbling stream runs forever
In the cave a clay pot boils over a fire on the ground
A wandering breeze stirs the fragrant pines
When hungry I eat one simple meal
And lean against the rock in complete harmony

Someone sits in a mountain vale
A robe of clouds, rainbows for tassels
The fragrant forest is the place to live
The road has been long and difficult
With a heart full of doubt and regret
A life has passed and nothing is accomplished
Others call it failure
I stand alone devoted to this Cold Mountain life

If you want a peaceful place to dwell
Cold Mountain is guaranteed forever
A light wind blows softly in the pines
The sound is good when you are close
One old man sits beneath the trees
Reading Lao Tzu and Huang Ti, mumbling
I could not find the world if I searched ten years
I've forgotten the road by which I came

The green stream runs very clear
Cold Mountain is silver white
Meditate and all becomes clear
Heaven is within

Sitting quietly alone before the cliff
The round moon is bright in the sky
Ten thousand things appear
Not one thing has a shadow or reflection
Spirit is very clear
Mysterious this empty cave
I point and look at the moon
The moon is all my heart really wants

How many autumns have I stayed at Cold Mountain
Singing to myself without worry or care
When hungry I eat one sutra
And lean against the rock contented

When people look for the road in the clouds
The cloud road disappears
The mountains are tall and steep
The streams are wide and still
Green mountains ahead and behind
White clouds to east and west
If you want to find the cloud road
Seek it within

***

The higher the trail the steeper it grows
Ten thousand tiers of dangerous cliffs
The stone bridge is slippery with green moss
Cloud after cloud keeps flying by
Waterfalls hang like ribbons of silk
The moon shines down on a bright pool
I climb the highest peak once more
To wait where the lone crane flies

Do I have a body? Or have I none?
Am I who I am? Or am I not?
Pondering these questions, I sit
Leaning against the cliff while the years go by
And the green grass grows up between my feet
And the red dust settles on my head
Then men of the world come and thinking me dead
Bring offerings of wine and fruit

My home used to be Cold Mountain
Resting among rocky cliffs far from worry or care
In the end the ten thousand things leave no trace
Now awake I wander the big thousand
Dancing light and shadow reflected in my mind
A single truth appeared
I realized my Buddha nature
Then everything changed

I sit cross-legged on the rock
The valleys and streams are cold and damp
Sitting quietly is beautiful
The cliffs are lost in mist and fog
I rest happily in this place
At dusk the tree shadows are low
I look into my mind
A lotus emerges from the dark mud

My five word poems total hundreds
Seven word seventy-nine
Three word twenty-one
Altogether maybe 600 poems
All written on ancient rocks
Boasting, my brushwork is strong
Who understands my poems
Is the mother of Buddha

*If your house has Cold Mountain poems
They're better for you than sutras
Hang them up where you can see them
Read them and read them again*

www.ingramcontent.com/pod-product-compliance
Lightning Source LLC
Chambersburg PA
CBHW022111090426
42743CB00008B/805